FAST FACTS

Indispensable
Guides to
Clinical
Practice

Stress and Strain

Second edition

James Campbell Quick

Professor of Organizational Behavior
The University of Texas at Arlington
Arlington, Texas, USA

Cary L Cooper

Professor of Organizational Psychology and Health

Fast Facts – Stress and Strain
First published 1999
Second edition September 2003

Text © 2003 James Campbell Quick and Cary L Cooper
© 2003 in this edition Health Press Limited
Elizabeth House, Queen Street, Abingdon, Oxford OX14 3JR, UK
Tel: +44 (0)1235 523233 Fax: +44 (0)1235 523238

Book orders can be placed by telephone or via the website.
For regional distributors or to order via the website, please go to:
www.fastfacts.com
For telephone orders, please call 01752 202301 (UK) or
1 800 538 1287 (North America, toll free).

Fast Facts is a trademark of Health Press Limited.

The publisher and the authors have made every effort to ensure the
accuracy of this book, but cannot accept responsibility for any errors or
omissions.

James Campbell Quick and Cary L Cooper would like to thank
Jonathan D Quick MD MPH, G Tyge Payne PhD, Neil H Dishon MD,
Kenneth Farr PhD and Frank Calhoun RPH for their professional advice
in the development of this work.

Registered names, trademarks, etc. used in this book, even when not
marked as such, are not to be considered unprotected by law.

A CIP catalogue record for this title is available from the British Library.

ISBN 1-903734-40-1

Library of Congress Cataloging-in-Publication Data

Quick, JC (James)
Fast Facts – Stress and Strain/
James Campbell Quick, Cary L Cooper

Illustrated by Dee McLean, London, UK.
Typeset by Zed, Oxford, UK.
Printed by Fine Print (Services), Oxford, UK.

Printed with vegetable inks on fully biodegradable and
recyclable paper manufactured from sustainable forests.

Low emissions
during production

Low
chlorine

Sustainable
forests

0613

Glossary

DSM-IV: *Diagnostic and Statistical Manual of Mental Disorders*, 4th edition

Eustress: the healthy, positive, constructive outcome of stressful events and the stress response

Job stress: the mind–body arousal resulting from physical and/or psychological stressors associated with a job and work

Medical management: tertiary prevention and treatment of strain based on medications, physical therapy and surgery

Preventive management: an approach and set of principles for promoting eustress and health while preventing strain and dysfunction

Primary prevention: the preventive management of stress by modifying, reducing, or altering stressors

Psychological management: tertiary prevention and treatment of strain based on psychotherapy, behavior therapy and traumatic event debriefing

Post-traumatic stress disorder (PTSD): a condition characterized by the reliving of an extremely traumatic event, accompanied by the symptoms of increased arousal and avoidance of stimuli associated with the trauma

Secondary prevention: the preventive management of stress by modifying, altering or changing the person's stress response to inevitable or unalterable stressors

Strain: the physiological, psychological and/or behavioral deviation from an individual's healthy functioning (synonymous with distress)

Stress management methods: methods for preventing strain while enhancing eustress

Stress response: the generalized, patterned, unconscious mobilization of the body's natural energy resources when confronted with a stressor

Stressor: a physical or psychological stimulus to which an individual responds (synonymous with demand)

Tertiary prevention: preventive management by treatment intervention to heal a person's strain

Trauma: a highly stressful, deeply disturbing or dramatically unexpected stressful event experienced as traumatic by the individual

Type A behavior pattern: a behavior–personality complex with the predominant features of competitive overdrive, devotion to work, anger–aggression and time urgency

Introduction

The stress response is a normal psychophysiological response to stressful or traumatic events, environmental stressors and interpersonal conflicts experienced by an individual. Stress poses a risk to health when it occurs frequently or is intense, prolonged or mismanaged. Stressful events can pose a threat to both health and life. Stress, although not the only or primary cause, is implicated in over half of all human morbidity and mortality. In the USA and developed countries, the ten leading causes of death account for 79–80% of all deaths (Figure 1). Stress is directly implicated in four causes (heart disease, strokes, injuries, and suicide and homicide) and indirectly implicated in a further three (cancer, chronic liver disease, and emphysema and chronic bronchitis). Common presenting symptoms are anxiety and depression.

Extensive research on stress, most notably in the past 30 years, has significantly increased our understanding of the role of stress in health

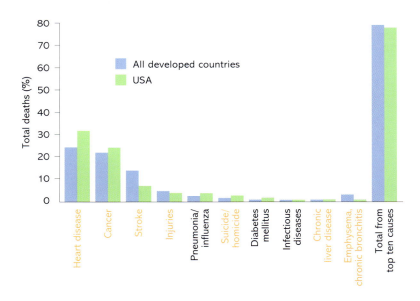

Figure 1 In 1990, stress was implicated in seven (highlighted in orange) of the ten leading causes of death in the developed world.

as well as in specific disorders and diseases. This scientific understanding has been translated and communicated to patients, dramatically increasing their awareness of stress. Consequently, family physicians and patients need to develop a greater understanding of stress and its implications, both in the short and long term.

Family physicians are seeing an increasing number of patients with stress-related anxiety and depression, and with chronic medical illnesses and psychological disorders that have a stress component. Stress-related disorders, and in particular anxiety and depression, continue to carry stigmas for many patients and some physicians. *Fast Facts – Stress and Strain* offers a concise overview of the psychophysiology of stress, the symptoms of stress-related disorders, the diagnosis of stress and strain, and the preventive management of stress and treatment of strain. The up-to-date, practical information provided here will help doctors and patients to reach appropriate decisions about long-term preventive strategies and short-term treatment options. Family physicians will also benefit from forming partnerships with mental health professionals in the diagnosis and treatment of stress-related disorders, because stress is a multidisciplinary concern.

Key references

Cooper C. *Theories of Organizational Stress*. Oxford: Oxford University Press, 1998.

Murray CJL. Global and regional cause-of-death patterns in 1990. In: *Global Comparative Assessments in the Health Sector*. Geneva: WHO, 1994:33–4.

World Health Organization. *World Health Statistics Annual 1993*. Geneva: WHO, 1994:D114–17.

The stress response is one element of the stress process. It consists of a generalized pattern of psychophysiological reactions triggered by stressors such as pressure, conflict or trauma (Figure 1.1). In contrast to more specific medical conditions, stress is a systemic mind–body response activated by the combined actions of the sympathetic nervous system and the endocrine system (Figure 1.2). The stress response is implicated in a range of chronic medical, behavioral and psychological disorders, and has four combined effects.

- Blood flow is redirected from the skin, intestines and other vegetative organs to the muscles and brain.
- Glucose and fatty acids are mobilized from storage sites into the bloodstream to provide readily available energy.
- Alertness is increased through a sharpening of sensory processes, such as vision and hearing.
- Functioning of the immune system, restorative processes and routine maintenance functioning, such as digestion, is reduced (Figure 1.3).

These effects have an important role at times of emergency and in stressful situations, yet pose a risk to health if they are sustained over a prolonged period, or elicited frequently or at a high intensity.

The sympathetic nervous system

The somatic nervous system controls skeletal muscle, and the autonomic nervous system controls the visceral organs. The autonomic

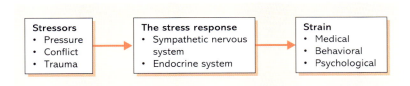

Figure 1.1 The stress process begins with a stressor such as pressure, conflict or trauma and may end with one or more manifestations of medical, behavioral or psychological strain.

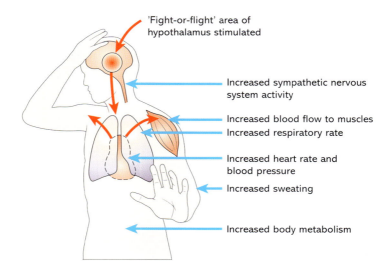

'Fight-or-flight' area of hypothalamus stimulated

Increased sympathetic nervous system activity

Increased blood flow to muscles

Increased respiratory rate

Increased heart rate and blood pressure

Increased sweating

Increased body metabolism

Figure 1.2 The physiological changes resulting from the stress response.

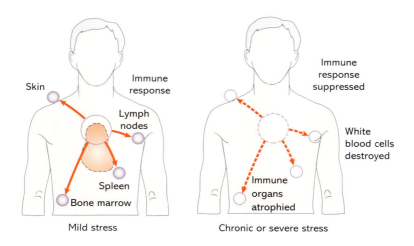

Skin

Immune response

Lymph nodes

Spleen

Bone marrow

Mild stress

Immune response suppressed

White blood cells destroyed

Immune organs atrophied

Chronic or severe stress

Figure 1.3 Immune system changes under stress. Under mild stress, the immune response is triggered and the heart's moderately increased pumping activates the skin, lymph nodes, spleen and bone marrow. Under chronic or severe stress, the immune response is suppressed or reduced. Immune organs atrophy and white cells are destroyed.

nervous system comprises the sympathetic nervous system, which is central to activating functions such as the stress response, and the parasympathetic nervous system, which is key to vegetative or healing activities as well as the relaxation response. The stress response has a systemic action that affects many of the body's organs (Figure 1.4). Typical manifestations of the stress response, such as increased alertness, nervousness and a pounding heart, are widely recognized (Table 1.1).

Catecholamines, primarily epinephrine (adrenaline) and norepinephrine (noradrenaline), are released into the bloodstream, causing sympathetic activity. In turn, catecholamine release has a direct activating effect on the central nervous system and, in particular, the

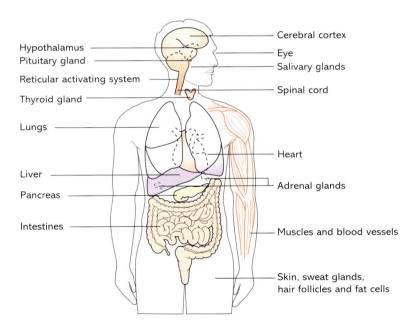

Figure 1.4 The stress response is generalized and affects a large number of bodily organs and systems. Source: Quick JC et al. *Preventive Stress Management in Organizations*. Washington, DC: APA. 1997:44. Copyright © 1997 by the American Psychological Association. Adapted with permission.

TABLE 1.1

The effects of the sympathetic nervous system on the body

Organ	Action of sympathetic nervous system	Manifest result
Brain (central nervous system)	Generalized stimulation	Increased alertness; nervousness
Eye	Dilated pupils	Wide-eyed appearance
Salivary glands	Reduced and thickened saliva	Dry mouth
Heart	Increased heart rate; increased force of contraction; increased volume of blood pumped	Palpitations; pounding heart
Lungs	Relaxed bronchi and increased respiration	Hyperventilation; sensation of shortness of breath (paradoxical)
Stomach and intestines	Decreased blood flow; decreased digestive activity and secretion	Queasy stomach; gnawing feeling in pit of stomach; nausea; constipation; paradoxical diarrhea occasionally
Liver	Release of glucose into bloodstream	Increased blood sugar (hyperglycemia)
Adrenal medulla	Stimulated secretion of epinephrine and norepinephrine	Potentiates all other sympathetic effects
Skin	Decreased blood flow	Pallor
Sweat glands	Increased sweating in selected areas, thick odorous secretions from oil glands	Sweaty palms and brow, possible worsening of skin conditions, body odor
Hair follicles	Piloerection	Goose bumps; hair stands on end
Blood vessels	Constricted blood vessels in skin, intestines and lungs	Hypertension
Muscles	Increased blood flow; increased excitability	Muscle tremors
Fat cells	Release of fatty acids into bloodstream	None

Source: Quick JC et al. *Preventive Stress Management in Organizations.* Washington, DC: APA, 1997:46. Copyright © 1997 by the American Psychological Association. Adapted with permission.

reticular activating system (RAS) or reticular formation. The RAS has a deep, central location in the brain, and was one of the earliest parts of the brain to evolve. It is concerned with level of consciousness, and stimulation leads to the awake, alert state associated with stressful situations.

The endocrine system

The most important hormones associated with stress are:

- adrenocorticotropic hormone (ACTH)
- cortisol
- glucagon
- epinephrine
- norepinephrine.

Adrenocorticotropic hormone. Within seconds of a person encountering an emergency or a stressful situation, a message is transmitted from the cerebral cortex to the hypothalamus and then to the pituitary gland. The pituitary gland releases ACTH, which acts on the adrenal cortex of the kidney to stimulate the conversion of cholesterol to steroid hormones, and the release of cortisol and glucocorticoids. It also causes mineralocorticoids, including aldosterone, to be released. Mineralocorticoids help to regulate blood pressure by causing the kidney to retain salt, thereby increasing blood pressure. Although ACTH is not the primary stimulant for aldosterone release, persistently high levels can lead to increased blood pressure.

Cortisol. Levels of glucose and fatty acids in the bloodstream are increased by cortisol. It also has a direct effect on a number of organs. For example, it:

- stimulates the liver to produce and release glucose
- stimulates fat cells to release fat
- causes tissues such as the skin to use less glucose.

Cortisol has several other effects on the body that can sometimes be quite harmful, including:

- causing the breakdown of protein for energy
- inhibiting immune and inflammatory responses

- causing lymphoid tissue to shrink
- weakening bones.

Moderate levels of cortisol can strengthen muscle contraction, but prolonged or excessive levels can weaken muscles. Large doses of cortisol, such as those used to treat certain inflammatory diseases, can cause psychosis or other mental changes.

Glucagon, like insulin, is released from the pancreas; it stimulates increased blood glucose and the release of fatty acids. In addition, it causes a slight increase in the rate and strength of the heartbeat.

Epinephrine and norepinephrine act both as hormones and as transmitters for the sympathetic nervous system.

Other hormones. Although thyroid hormone and growth hormone have other primary functions, they are also stimulated by stress.

Pathways to strain

In the stress response, the sympathetic nervous system and endocrine system work concurrently to mobilize the body's resources. Increased epinephrine release has immediate behavioral and psychological consequences, the most predominant effects being heightened alertness and a sense of apprehension. Although these effects can be useful in

---

Key points – Psychophysiology of stress

- The stress response activates the mind and body for peak performance when coping with emergencies.
- The sympathetic nervous system and the endocrine system are both activated by stress.
- Key changes include increased muscle tension, modified blood flow, release of body fuels, increased alertness and decreased immune function.
- Stress poses a risk and becomes a problem when it is not well managed.

emergency situations, the cardiovascular and metabolic effects of stress can result in many adverse medical consequences. Stress poses a generalized rather than a specific health risk. A person may experience a range of medical, psychological and/or behavioral disorders, depending on their particular vulnerabilities. A family history that charts disorders and diseases can help to identify potential pathways that may culminate in strain for any individual.

Key references

Cannon WB. *The Wisdom of the Body.* New York: Norton, 1932.

Cooper C, Palmer S. *Conquer Your Stress.* London: Chartered Institute of Personnel Development, 2001.

Cooper CL, ed. *Handbook of Stress, Medicine, and Health.* Boca Raton: CRC Press, 1996.

Cooper CL, Dewe P, O'Driscoll M. *Organizational Stress.* Thousand Oaks, CA: Sage Publishing, 2001.

Cooper KH. *Can Stress Heal?* Nashville: Thomas Nelson, 1997.

Quick JC, Quick JD, Nelson DL et al. *Preventive Stress Management in Organizations.* Washington: American Psychological Association, 1997.

Selye H. *Stress in Health and Disease.* Boston: Butterworth, 1976.

Wolff HG. *Stress and Disease.* Springfield: Charles C Thomas, 1953.

2 Stress-related disorders and individual differences

Although there is no inherent pathology associated with the stress response, stress presents a generalized health risk factor and is implicated in a wide range of medical, psychological and behavioral disorders. This chapter identifies the types of disorders in which stress is directly or indirectly implicated. Many systems within the body are susceptible to the stress response. The manifestations of strain experienced by an individual reflect his or her particular weakness or unique vulnerability. This organ inferiority hypothesis suggests that, under the same stressful conditions, one person may experience gastrointestinal distress, while another may experience cardiovascular distress, a third person may have vasorespiratory distress and a fourth may experience skin or general metabolism disorders. Several individual differences influence this vulnerability and are modifiers of the stress response.

Presenting complaints and early warning signs

The most common presenting complaints to family physicians for stress and stress-related health problems are generalized anxiety and depression. The significant increase in anxiety over the past half-century has two primary causes:

- the increase in environmental threats, such as civil crimes, domestic conflicts and terrorist activities
- the decrease in social connectedness and secure interpersonal attachments within the population, as exemplified by social isolation of the aged or the loneliness of latch-key children in homes where both parents are at work and no caretaker is available.

Both of these causes also contribute to the experience of depression.

The US Federal Bureau of Investigation estimates that a stressful event is most frequently the triggering event in cases of workplace violence. While workplace violence is a publicly visible traumatic event, domestic violence is much more likely to be hidden and is therefore more difficult to identify, yet it is a serious risk to personal well-being for some and a public health menace for all.

The presenting complaints of generalized anxiety and depression are often accompanied by a number of more specific complaints that constitute early warning signs. Family physicians should look for the following early warning signs of strain and presenting complaints of stress-related disorders:

- insomnia and sleep disturbances
- inability to focus and concentrate
- fatigue and general irritability
- muscle tension and pain
- heart palpitations
- stomach upset and gastrointestinal problems.

Case report 2.1

Mrs D, a 24-year-old graduate student, presented to her physician with insomnia and forgetfulness that was interfering with her studies. There were no accompanying medical indications. A patient history indicated no previous occurrence of these symptoms during development. A stress diagnostic profile was developed by asking questions about her university activities and home environment. The profile provided evidence of a new and happy marriage without children, and revealed no indications of unusual stressors or pressures within the university environment.

Mrs D was asked to keep a diary at the end of each day for a month, writing down all of her thoughts and feelings about the day's activities. Subsequent examination of the diary revealed the presence of many negative words and thoughts, expressions of fears and anxieties, and pessimistic thinking. Mrs D was then taught and read about learned optimism (see Chapter 5). By developing the habit of non-negative thinking through learned optimism, Mrs D's insomnia and forgetfulness were relieved.

In addition, up to 25% of patients with stress-related problems may have suicidal thoughts. Psychosomatic complaints have a stress-related component, and organic bases for the complaints must be ruled out at the outset of treatment.

Individual differences

Several individual differences influence the stress process and create vulnerabilities for, or protection against, stress-related disorders. The four main individual differences are gender, type A behavior pattern (stress propensity), family history and emotional intelligence.

Women have a tendency to 'tend-and-befriend' (in other words, form positive supports) under stressful conditions. They are therefore less vulnerable to fatal and violent forms of strain, such as heart attacks and physical, anger-based conflict. However, women are at greater risk of depression (which may sometimes lead to suicide) and other non-fatal forms of strain.

Type A behavior pattern is an individual difference that creates stress vulnerability. The absence of this behavior pattern, also known as type B behavior pattern, creates protection against stress-related disorders. This has been known since about 1860, when the Dutch cardiologist Von Dusch first identified excessive work involvement as creating cardiovascular risk, which is affected by stress.

Family history can help to identify vulnerability to various types of stress-related disorders, as well as to identify protection factors. Taking a careful personal and family health history from patients yields rich information.

Finally, emotions are central to stimulation of the stress response. Cannon focused on fear and rage as two key emotions causing stress. Individuals with greater emotional intelligence, which is the ability to identify one's own emotions and those of other people, are better able to manage and process fear, rage and other emotions without adverse stress-related effects in their mind, body or behavior. Hence, questioning patients about their behavior, family history and emotions can be helpful in gaining some information about individual differences.

Symptoms and early warning signs may be either chronic or episodic in nature. The former may arise from unresolved emotions and feelings related to stressful events or traumas that occurred several months to years previously. (Chronic musculoskeletal pains and tensions may, however, be related to mechanical problems in the use of arms and legs.) More recent and specific stressful events or traumas may trigger episodic symptoms. The underlying causes of stress and stress-related disorders are discussed in greater depth in Chapter 3.

Stress-related disorders

Early warning signs, symptoms and asymptomatic risk factors can lead to frank and serious strain. Stress-related disorders fall into three broad categories: medical, psychological and behavioral. Because stress is a generalized, systemic response of the mind–body, it is not easy to predict which category of stress-related disorder a specific patient may manifest.

In addition to early warning signs and symptoms, the physician should be concerned about long-term major health problems to which stress may be a contributory factor. A family medical history can be useful in identifying a person's probable vulnerability to major stress-related health disorders. This is most notable in cases of hypertension and cardiovascular disease. Compiling individual case histories covering several family generations, including major health problems, ages and causes of death, will often reveal major health risks (Figure 2.1). A family history may highlight a predisposing factor based on the organ inferiority hypothesis, but it cannot predict whether or not an individual will develop a particular problem.

Medical strain. Stress is implicated in or a direct contributing factor to at least five common and sometimes serious forms of medical strain (Table 2.1). While these medical conditions may have other primary or secondary causes, each may have a stress-related component.

Cardiovascular disease may occur because the cardiovascular system is involved in the stress response. Although there is no evidence that stress plays a role in the development of atherosclerosis, stress is implicated in sudden-death heart attacks and hypertension (Figure 2.2). Several physiologically normal cardiovascular aspects of the stress response can become physiologically abnormal if the stress is particularly intense, frequent or of prolonged duration.

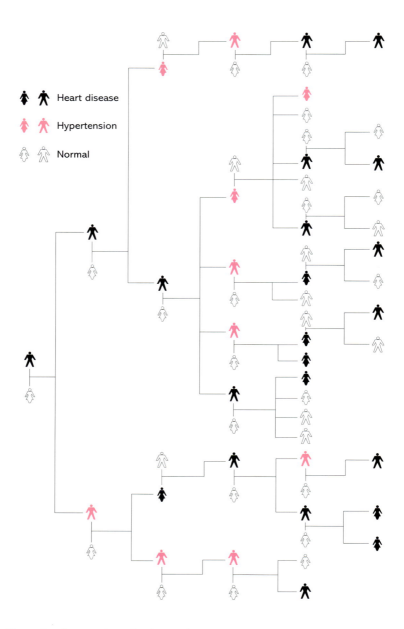

Figure 2.1 Constructing a family tree that charts disorders and diseases may reveal a likely manifestation of stress for an individual, such as heart disease.

TABLE 2.1

Symptoms of medical strain arising from stress

- Cardiovascular disease, including hypertension, elevated heart rate and blood pressure; increased risk of heart attack during extreme stress; type A (coronary-prone) behavior creates self-induced stress

- Back pain triggers a bracing response in the large muscles, causing contraction and tension, particularly in the muscles of the back, abdomen and upper thighs

- Tension headaches may be of musculoskeletal origin from the contraction of the large muscles in the upper back, shoulders, neck and scalp

- Cancer is indirectly influenced by stress; there may be predisposition to possible malignancy because of lowered immunity; stress can inhibit the curative process

- Stress is thought to be a factor in irritable bowel syndrome and is possibly implicated in peptic ulcer disease

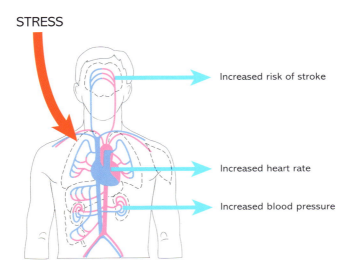

Figure 2.2 The effects of stress on the cardiovascular system may lead to heart attack and hypertension.

Case report 2.2

Reverend H, aged 56 years, reported to a cardiologist that he was experiencing chest pains, frequently on Saturday afternoons and evening, but also at other times of the week. A complete diagnostic work-up and tests provided no evidence of heart disease or high blood pressure. A stress diagnostic profile was developed by asking questions about work activities and the home environment. The profile provided no evidence of undue pressures within the home environment. However, it identified that the church for which Reverend H was head of staff was in a period of major expansion and activities related to this expansion were placing time pressures on his sermon preparation. Hence, the two primary stressors in his work life were work overload from the church expansion and the time pressures this caused. The church staff structure did not allow for additional delegation of activities and Reverend H already had well-developed time management skills.

Following the negative physiological test results and the positive identification of workplace stressors, Reverend H made a career change decision that placed him in a smaller, stable church that was not intending to grow. His chest pains stopped with the change in pastorates.

Chronic back pain is the most common cause of chronic disability within the working population. It is particularly likely to occur in people who have jobs that expose the lower back to risk of injury (e.g. laborers and truck drivers). Prolonged stress contributes directly to over 50% of chronic back pain problems.

Headaches can be caused by stress, tension, genetic vulnerability or organic disorder, and diagnosis must separate out those that are related to stress and tension. Migraine headaches are organic in origin, and stress plays only a minor role.

Cancer is not caused by stress. However, established risk factors for cancer include a number of forms of behavioral strain, such as tobacco and alcohol abuse. Occupational risks, such as exposure to chemicals and radiation, are likely to be higher in people whose sleep pattern and concentration is disturbed, because they are already stressed by lack of sleep and are also more likely to be accident-prone. Stress-related inhibition of the immune reponse may also be a factor.

Some gastrointestinal conditions are thought to be associated with stress, including irritable bowel syndrome.

Psychological strain. Psychology plays a central role in the stress process, and physicians should consider partnering with mental health professionals whenever stress-related problems of a more serious nature are suspected. Stressful events, chronic stress and trauma are all important health risks for psychological strain (Table 2.2).

Depression is the most common, significant psychological condition seen by family physicians. Fortunately, with a combination of pharmacological intervention and psychotherapy, depression is also one of the most treatable psychological problems. Stressful life events may trigger a depression, and these lift with time. Bipolar or manic depression is a possible diagnosis for patients who experience cycles of highs and lows unrelated to stressful life circumstances or events.

TABLE 2.2

Symptoms of psychological strain arising from stress

- Varying degrees of depression
- Burnout from chronic stress and prolonged striving can lead to emotional exhaustion and reduced personal accomplishment
- Anxiety disorders may develop, including acute stress disorder, post-traumatic stress disorder, panic disorder, agoraphobia, social phobia, obsessive–compulsive disorder and generalized anxiety disorder
- Conversion reactions can trigger psychogenic conditions, such as acute blindness and hand or arm paralysis
- Work–family stress may trigger interpersonal conflicts, physical abuse or sexual dysfunction

Burnout can result from chronic levels of high stress and striving, often manifesting itself as fatigue and lack of energy. Emotional exhaustion is very often at the core of burnout. Those most at risk of burnout are people who are under pressure to achieve within their job and those with caregiving roles receiving limited support.

Anxiety disorders affect one in every six people in the USA and one in every five employed people in the UK, and include a wide range of stress-related disorders (Table 2.2). Anxiety and nervous debility account for about one in three consultations with family physicians. Diagnosis and treatment of these forms of psychological strain have improved recently.

Conversion reactions occur when the mind affects the body's functioning. Severe psychogenic physical disability may result, such as acute blindness or paralysis of a hand or arm. The pathways via which conversion reactions occur are not often clear. Somatization disorders – the experience of multiple unexplained physical symptoms – are a related form of psychological strain.

Family problems may lead to several manifestations of psychological strain. Some people find balancing work and family life extremely stressful.

Behavioral strain. Behavioral forms of strain are most often dysfunctional attempts to cope with stress and trauma (Table 2.3).

Substance abuse is associated with stress. The use of tobacco products is the single most preventable cause of death. Smoking appears to increase with the number of stressors on a given person for a discrete period of time. Excess alcohol consumption is also associated with substantial personal and social costs. In the USA, alcohol abuse is implicated in half of all road traffic accidents, motor vehicle fatalities and manslaughters, and one-third of reported suicides. In the UK, the British Medical Association has estimated that either the offender or the victim has been drinking in 65% of homicides, 75% of stabbings, 70% of beatings and 50% of fights or cases of domestic violence. UK data also suggest that 65% of suicides are linked to excessive drinking. A key factor in drug-taking behavior is self-medication for stress-related problems and occupational difficulties.

TABLE 2.3

Behavioral forms of strain

- Substance abuse: tobacco, alcohol and drugs
- Violence, manslaughter and suicide
- Increased susceptibility to accidents
- Prolonged recovery times from accidents and injuries
- Eating disorders: overeating leads to obesity, with its associated cardiovascular and musculoskeletal problems; undereating may result from loss of appetite, which is often associated with depression

The abuse of drugs, prescription or illegal, can have long-term adverse consequences.

Violence may be verbal or physical. It can also be manifest in self-destructive forms. Anger and hostility in response to stress are among the precursors to aggressive and violent behavior. In the USA, homicide is the leading cause of death among women in the workplace. The British Crime Survey of 1998 estimated that 3.3 million work-hours had been lost that year due to violence. Furthermore, a large-scale Norwegian survey found that 40% of people who had experienced work-place violence had contemplated suicide as a consequence.

Industrial accidents are the leading cause of death for men at work in the USA. Automobile drivers who experience stressful social or job-associated events are five times more likely to cause a fatal accident than drivers not experiencing such stress.

Eating disorders are also a manifestation of behavioral strain.

Key points – Stress-related disorders and individual difference

- Generalized anxiety and depression are the most common presenting complaints of stressed patients.
- Early warning signs are important because stress poses a chronic health risk.
- Gender, type A behavior personality, family history and emotional intelligence are individual differences that can influence the stress process.
- Advanced medical strain may manifest as cardiovascular disease, chronic back pain, or headaches, or may contribute to advancing cancers.
- Advanced psychological strain may manifest as burnout, conversion reactions, anxiety disorders or family problems.
- Advanced behavioral strain may manifest as substance abuse, violent behavior, eating disorders or accident-prone behavior.

Key references

Branch CL, Gates RL, Susman JL et al. *Low Back Pain.* Monograph No. 185. Kansas City: American Academy of Family Physicians, 1994.

Cannon WB. *Bodily Changes in Pain, Hunger, Fear and Rage. An Account of Recent Researches into The Function of Emotional Excitement.* 2nd edn. New York and London: D Appleton-Century, 1934 [original work, 1915].

Cooper CL, Watson M. *Cancer and Stress: Psychological, Biological, and Coping studies.* Chichester: Wiley, 1991.

Di Martino V, Hole H, Cooper CL. *Preventing Violence and Harrassment in the Workplace.* Dublin: European Foundation for the Improvement in Living and Working Conditions, 2003.

Hammar N, Alfredsson L, Theorell T. Job characteristics and incidence of myocardial infarction. *Int J Epidemiol* 1994;28:277–84.

Marsella AJ, Friedman MJ, Gerrity ET et al., eds. *Ethnocultural Aspects of Posttraumatic Stress Disorder: Issues, Research, and Clinical Applications.* Washington: American Psychological Association, 1996.

Maslach C. *Burnout: The Cost of Caring*. Englewood Cliffs: Prentice-Hall, 1982.

National Safety Council. *Accident Facts*. Chicago: National Safety Council, 1990.

Stallones L, Kraus JF. The occurrence and epidemiologic features of alcohol-related occupational injuries. *Addiction* 1993; 88:945–51.

Van den Bos GR, Bulatao EQ, eds. *Violence on the Job: Identifying Risks and Developing Solutions*. Washington: American Psychological Association, 1996.

Wolf S, Wolff HG. *Gastric Function: an Experimental Study of a Man and his Stomach*. New York: Oxford University Press, 1943.

Three general guidelines exist for a physician when diagnosing stress.

- Symptoms and complaints not of a specific organic basis should be identified in the diagnostic process, such as chest pains in the absence of organic cardiovascular disease.
- The physician should look for complaints or symptoms that are an overreaction or prolonged reaction to stressors or traumatic life events.
- Stress diagnosis is sometimes complicated by the overlap of stress-related disorders with more basic psychological disorders – in such cases, a knowledgeable mental health professional is required.

Evaluating causes and high-risk situations

While many health problems and diseases have a specific cause or, at most, a limited set of specific causes and risk factors, stress and stress-related disorders are not diagnosed in quite the same way. The key to the stress diagnostic process is careful examination of the patient's work and personal environments to identify the stressors, traumas and tensions that might underlie the presenting symptoms. The physician should be looking for specific relationships, working conditions, specific jobs, or personal losses and traumas at the root of the symptoms. Hence, stress diagnosis is a rather broad-based, 'open-lens' process of seeking out the sources of stress that are triggering the symptoms presented.

The important diagnostic process to pursue in all cases is to move from the generalized set of symptoms and less specific presenting complaints of anxiety or depression (see below) to a better defined cause or set of causes for the stress. Once this is identified, it may be highly appropriate for the family physician to function as a triage agent by engaging other appropriate professionals or resources to help the patient learn new skills for addressing the sources of stress.

In addition to reviewing the patient's current personal and work life domains, the physician should be very attentive to life history events that may be the cause of the problems, especially events that occurred in the previous 12–18 months. There is substantial medical and psychological evidence indicating that major life changes pose a high stress-related health risk for a period of 12–18 months following the event.

Diagnostic instruments. Two excellent diagnostic instruments for stress and stress-related disorders are the Stress and Coping Inventory and ASSET. The former is more oriented to the patient's personal life, but does consider the work arena and also provides information about strengths as well as risks and vulnerabilities. The latter diagnostic tool has a more occupational orientation.

The Stress and Coping Inventory (Health Assessment Programs Inc., USA) can provide both the physician and patient with useful stress diagnostic information about:

- stress and strain, including recent life changes, physical and psychological symptoms, and behaviors and emotions
- coping resources, including health habits, social support, responses to stress, life satisfactions, purpose and connection
- stress and coping balance.

The Brief Stress and Coping Inventory is a shorter, self-scoring version of this tool.

ASSET – An Organizational Stress Screening Tool (www.robertsoncooper.com) provides the occupational health physician and client with a psychometrically robust stress diagnostic instrument with an occupational orientation. It can be completed on-line or paper-and-pencil computer read, and assesses:

- sources of pressure, including work relationships, work–life balance, overload, job security and control
- attitudes toward work, such as employee commitment
- effects of stress and pressure on physical health and psychological well-being.

Common sources of stress. There are several high-risk situations that should be probed with these diagnostic instruments and by other means. These include major life changes, difficult relationships and high-risk working conditions.

Major life changes may fall into several important categories, including traumatic events, personal losses and job changes.

- Traumatic events, for example caused by domestic violence, are significant because they interrupt the patient's healthy habits of living and require considerable effort to make necessary adjustments.
- Personal losses also constitute a form of stressful trauma with associated deep emotional pain.
- Job loss, demotion or transition is also a major life-changing event that causes stress and requires adjustment.

The degree of health risk associated with these life changes depends in part on the healthy habits, coping strategies and preventive management practices already used by the patient at the time of the event. These strength factors help to offset the risks associated with the stressful events.

Difficult relationships, either at work or at home, constitute another major cause of stress. While some conflict is a normal and at times a healthy characteristic of human relationships, chronic and unresolved conflicts that characterize a difficult relationship are causes of significant personal stress and pose a serious health risk for the patient. For example, difficult relationships are a known cause of cardiovascular irregularities and symptoms. In extreme cases, there is a risk of death by violence.

Job stress is the leading stress factor for many patients in the USA and the UK. The sources of job stress are risk of job loss, work overload, conflicts in the workplace, obsession or preoccupation with work, and computer work (due to repetitive motion problems, poor posture and learning new systems). The physician should seek to identify specific pressure points and sources of stress at work by using the ASSET instrument or taking a careful patient history. The purpose of seeking to identify the better-defined underlying causes of stress at work is that the patient may then have some intuitive as well as practical ideas for making adjustments or changes to alleviate the cause of the stress.

The Confederation of British Industries sickness absence survey (2000) found that workplace stress was the leading cause of sickness absence for non-manual employees. This workplace stress can lead to other outcomes such as accidents, drug and alcohol problems and poor workplace morale.

Stress-related symptoms

Common presenting complaints. The most common presenting stress-related complaints are generalized depression, generalized anxiety and panic attacks.

Generalized depression. Signs and symptoms of generalized depression include:

- depressed mood and feeling sad
- little interest or pleasure in activities previously enjoyed
- change in appetite or weight
- change in sleep habits
- restlessness or inactivity
- fatigue or loss of energy
- feeling worthless or guilty
- difficulty concentrating or making decisions
- thoughts of death or suicide.

Generalized anxiety is indicated by at least 6 months of persistent and excessive anxiety and worry.

Panic attacks are a more specific form of stress-related anxiety disorder and are characterized by a period of intense fear or discomfort, in which at least four of the following 13 symptoms develop abruptly and reach a peak within 10 minutes:

- palpitations, pounding heart or accelerated heart rate
- sweating
- trembling or shaking
- sensations of shortness of breath or smothering
- feelings of choking
- chest pain or discomfort
- nausea or abdominal discomfort
- feeling dizzy, unsteady, light-headed or faint
- derealization (feelings of unreality) or depersonalization (being detached)
- fear of losing control or going crazy

> ### Case report 3.1
>
> Captain P, aged 36 years, reported persistent feelings of generalized anxiety and tension following an assignment to a headquarters military unit. She had no accompanying medical indications. A patient history revealed no developmental history of anxiety problems, either in the military as an enlisted member and a lieutenant or prior to military service. A stress diagnostic profile was developed by asking questions about her new headquarters assignment and her home environment. The profile revealed that Captain P had a stable marriage without children, but high stress and pressure responsibilities at the headquarters military unit. This suggested that the generalized anxiety and tension were associated with the pressures of significantly increased work responsibilities.
>
> Captain P developed a program of expressive writing (see Chapter 5, Emotional outlets) in which she freely expressed her deepest and most emotional thoughts into her computer at the end of each day. This process provided an emotional outlet for her anxieties and tensions, enabling her to let go of the pressures that had previously been internalized. Captain P's anxiety and tension returned to normal levels within about a month or two, and her work performance never suffered.

- fear of dying
- paresthesias (numbness or tingling sensations)
- chills or hot flushes.

Post-traumatic stress disorder (PTSD) is a less common presenting complaint than generalized depression, generalized anxiety or panic attacks, but is nevertheless a diagnostically important stress-related condition. It is characterized by the reliving of an extremely traumatic event, accompanied by symptoms of increased arousal and avoidance of stimuli associated with the trauma. The DSM-IV (*Diagnostic and*

Statistical Manual of Mental Disorders – 4th edition) is a valuable resource for physicians in diagnosing PTSD. Mental health professionals can also assist in the diagnosis, as well as management, of this disorder.

TABLE 3.1

Behavioral symptoms of stress

- Constant irritability with people
- Difficulty in making decisions
- Loss of sense of humour
- Suppressed anger
- Difficulty in concentrating
- Inability to complete one task before rushing into another
- Feeling the target of other people's animosity
- Feeling unable to cope
- Wanting to cry at the smallest problem
- Lack of interest in pursuing activities outside of work
- Feeling tired after an early night
- Constant tiredness

TABLE 3.2

Physical symptoms of stress

- Lack of appetite
- Craving food when under pressure
- Frequent indigestion or heartburn
- Constipation or diarrhea
- Insomnia
- Tendency to sweat for no apparent reason
- Nervous twitches, nail biting, etc.
- Headaches
- Cramps and muscle spasms
- Nausea
- Breathlessness without exertion
- Fainting
- Impotence or frigidity
- Eczema

TABLE 3.3

Effects of stress on bodily functions

	Normal (relaxed)	**Under pressure**
Brain	Normal blood supply	Increased blood supply
Saliva	Normal	Reduced
Muscles	Normal blood supply	Increased blood supply
Heart	Normal heart rate and blood pressure	Increased heart rate and blood pressure
Lungs	Normal respiration	Increased respiration rate
Stomach	Normal blood supply and acid secretion	Reduced blood supply Increased acid secretion
Bowels	Normal	Reduced blood supply Increased bowel activity
Bladder	Normal	Frequent urination
Sexual organs	(M) Normal	(M) Impotence (decreased blood supply)
	(F) Normal periods	(F) Irregular periods
Skin	Healthy	Decreased blood supply
Biochemistry	Normal oxygen, glucose and fat consumption	Increased oxygen, glucose and fat consumption

F, female; M, male

Source: Melhuish A. *Executive Health*. Business Books, 1978. Adapted with the permission of The Random House Group Ltd, London, UK

Stages of stress-related symptoms. Stress-related symptoms are the outcome of an individual's failure to cope within a given environment. This is described by the physical and psychological symptoms associated with the exhaustion stage of Selye's General Adaptation Syndrome and the failure-to-cope adjustment process of the Cummings and Cooper model. There are three stages of symptoms that are reflected by these models.

First-stage symptoms. Initially, the individual tends to show behavioral symptoms of stress. The physician can identify these

Acute pressure	Chronic pressure (stress)
Think more clearly	Headaches and migraines, tremors and nervous tics
Reduced	Dry mouth, lump in throat
Improved performance	Muscular tension and pain
Improved performance	Hypertension and chest pain
Improved performance	Coughs and asthma
Decreased blood supply reduces digestion	Ulcers due to heartburn and indigestion
Decreased blood supply reduces digestion	Abdominal pain and diarrhea
Frequent urination due to increased nervous stimulation	Frequent urination, prostatic symptoms
Decreased blood supply	(M) Impotence (F) Menstrual disorders
Decreased blood supply	Dryness and rashes
More energy immediately available	Rapid tiredness

symptoms clinically by asking the patient about them in a medical history or interview, and looking in particular for changes in habits or routines. A certain amount of pressure may be stimulating and invigorating; however, when this pressure exceeds a level at which the individual is able to cope, it can be defined as stress. There are a number of behavioral symptoms associated with the early stage of the stress response (Table 3.1). The appearance of such symptoms usually means that the individual is no longer coping and has crossed the 'pressure–stress' divide.

Second-stage symptoms. If the original source of stress continues, the individual enters the second stage, which is usually indicated by minor physical symptoms (Table 3.2). Most individuals have a genetic and/or family susceptibility to stress. Excessive stress can sometimes result in a failing immune system, which can lead to symptoms such as frequent bouts of flu or colds, or other non-life-threatening microbiological manifestations (e.g. skin disorders). The body has a number of physiological responses to stress (Table 3.3).

Third-stage symptoms. The longer and more severe the source of stress, such as a bad and worsening marriage or prolonged illness of a loved one, and the fewer coping resources an individual has to deal with it, the worse and more serious the symptoms and potential consequences will be. For example, there is increasing evidence that stress may be a risk factor for heart disease, some immune system failures (e.g. chronic fatigue syndrome) and some forms of cancer. However, it is important that physicians eliminate an organic cause before making the clinical leap to a diagnosis of stress. Only after thorough diagnosis of other potential conditions should an exploration of the stress etiology of a physical manifestation be pursued. The physician can explore stress etiology by putting the patient's stressful

---

Key points – Diagnosing stress and symptoms of strain

- Stress diagnosis requires a broad scope of enquiry to identify underlying causes and high-risk situations.
- Two good stress diagnostic instruments are the Stress and Coping Inventory and the ASSET instrument.
- The primary presenting stress complaints are anxiety and depression.
- Strain may manifest as a wide range of medical or psychological disorders.
- Stress diagnosis is a multidisciplinary process requiring medical, psychological or other specialty expertise.

life events on a chart, or timeline, along with symptoms. Other possible sources of the physical symptoms, such as lifestyle factors (e.g. type A behavior), the presence of adverse life events and other psychosocial factors (e.g. lack of social support) can then be investigated.

Key references

American Psychiatric Association. *Diagnostic and Statistical Manual of Mental Disorders,* 4th edition *(DSM-*IV-TR*)*. Washington: American Psychiatric Association, 2000.

Barrow, JW. *Making Diagnosis Meaningful: Enhancing Evaluation and Treatment of Psychological Disorders.* Washington: American Psychological Association, 1998.

Baughan DM. Barriers to diagnosing anxiety disorders in family practice. *Am Fam Physician* 1995;52:447–50.

Cooper CL, Sloan SJ, Williams S. *Occupational Stress Indicator.* Windsor, UK: NFER-Nelson, 1988.

Cummings T, Cooper CL. A cybernetic theory of occupational stress. *Human Relations* 1979;32: 395–418.

Maslach C, Jackson SE. *Maslach Burnout Inventory.* Palo Alto, California: Consulting Psychologists Press, 1981.

Melhuish A. *Executive Health.* London: Business Books, 1978.

Quick JC, Quick JD. Daily log of stress-related symptoms. In: *Organizational Stress and Preventive Management.* New York: McGraw-Hill, 1984:130–3.

Selye H. The general adaptation syndrome and the diseases of adaptation. *J Clin Endocrinol* 1946;6:117.

Although a little stress can be good for most of us, the strain caused by chronic stress can give rise to various health problems, as described in previous chapters. Preventive and treatment strategies for the management of stress are therefore appropriate.

In the preventive management of stress, the following assumptions are made:

- stress is an inevitable experience related to life and work
- a certain level of stress is good
- strain is a preventable or treatable outcome of the stress process
- primary, secondary or tertiary prevention enhances eustress and reduces strain.

The preventive management of stress uses concepts from preventive medicine, and applies them to a stress process model (see Chapter 1).

It may be difficult for a physician to convince patients either to address underlying causes of their presenting strain or to acquire prevention practices aimed at averting future episodes of strain. These difficulties are related to the stigma attached to anxiety, depression and other stress-related disorders, and the common patient expectation that they should be able to cope without help.

The physician must therefore validate stress-related disorders as simply a health issue for which treatment and help are available. This is the first step for the patient in accepting the need to learn prevention skills to enable them to live with stress successfully.

Stages of chronic conditions

Chronic disorders do not arise suddenly. Rather, they develop gradually through a progression of stages or natural life history. The process can be broken down into the following stages:

- susceptibility
- early disease
- advanced or disabling disease.

The stages of a chronic condition can be illustrated by studying, for example, the disease path of coronary artery disease. At the stage of susceptibility, the individual is healthy and exposed to certain health risks or precursors to illness, such as a sedentary lifestyle or smoking. The development of atherosclerotic plaques is the early or preclinical disease, when few, if any, symptoms are present. As the disease advances to the final stage, it becomes symptomatic or clinical disease. Angina pectoris and heart attacks are advanced manifestations of coronary artery disease. By considering the life history of stress in the same way, different preventive strategies can be employed to manage the different stages (Figure 4.1).

Within the preventive medicine framework, stressors and trauma are considered to be health risks at the stage of susceptibility. The second stage is the stress response, which may or may not be a problem. If the individual's stress response is appropriate to the intensity, frequency or duration of the stressor, then this stage is not considered problematic. However, if the individual's stress response to the specific stressful event is too intense or prolonged, or alternatively, if the response is insufficient, this could be problematic, and cause progression to the third stage. Here, excessive or chronic stressors and/or individual

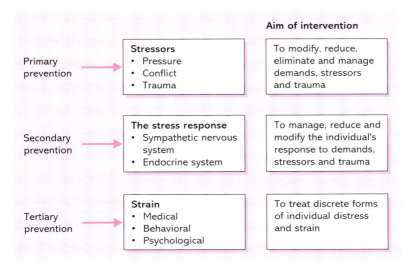

Figure 4.1 Stress can be considered a chronic health risk for which preventive medicine concepts may be applied.

difficulty in managing the stress response may lead to medical, psychological or behavioral strain. This strain is symptomatic and clinical in nature, and requires treatment intervention.

Natural protective and vulnerability factors

The progression of the stress response to strain is not inevitable. There is growing evidence that individuals have natural protective mechanisms and defences that enable them to maintain their health even when exposed to such risks. In contrast to this, individuals also have natural vulnerabilities that can be identified from their personal and family histories. With regard to preventive management of stress, there is strong evidence that individuals have both natural and learned protective factors which enable them to remain healthy during periods of high stress. The aim of preventive management is to build on patients' natural protective factors, as well as teaching them new methods and skills for preventive stress management.

Basic skills for preventive stress management

Physicians and patients alike may benefit from a set of basic skills related to preventive stress management. These generalized practical skills aim to build resilience, physiological balance and positive psychological energy in the individual who practices them. These basic skills are a solid foundation for a more comprehensive and personalized approach to preventive stress management using the specific skills of primary and secondary prevention, along with the appropriate use of tertiary prevention and treatment strategies for specific stress-related disorders, as discussed in Chapters 5 and 6. We emphasize the basic skills as essential and necessary, but not sufficient alone, for the successful and healthy management of stress.

The four essential basic skills are:
- diaphragmatic breathing
- flexibility practices
- humor skills
- positive respites.

The experience of stress demands energy expenditure, often at a very unconscious level. Because it elicits a fight-or-flight response, it places the patient in a struggle mode that must be counteracted through the use of generalized skills coupled with specific prevention practices aimed at channeling stress-induced energy in positive ways.

Diaphragmatic breathing – that is, slow, deep breathing from the abdomen – is a skill that patients can practice. It is especially useful in moments of anger or high emotion, because a slow, deep out-breath serves also to lower the heart rate. The effect of slowing the breathing and lowering the heart rate is to calm both the mind and the body. A related benefit is that the patient shifts their focus from the specific cause of stress to the way in which they are responding to the stressful situation. The patient should be cautioned that this is not a 'quick fix' therapy, but rather a life-long discipline that fundamentally enhances their health and calms their reactions. Additionally, once the discipline of good diaphragmatic breathing is learned, it can be used in the heat of a stressful moment to avert unhealthy, negative or destructive reactions. It is appropriate to suggest that the patient focuses attention on quiet diaphragmatic breathing at least twice each day for no less than 5 minutes at a time. It can be easily done at work or at home.

Flexibility practices constitute a generalized skill for dispelling stress and tension build-up in the large muscles of the body. Gently stretching the arms and legs, bending the head from side to side, rolling the shoulders and stretching the back sequentially is useful for alleviating tension in each of the large muscle groups of the body. Muscle tension build-up can be especially problematic for those who work at computer terminals and workstations for extended periods of time. Such patients should take stretch breaks every 30 minutes to 1 hour, or more frequently as required. Flexibility practices serve an important role in releasing the physical tension that inevitably results from stress.

Humor skills and mirthful laughter have been found to have generalized and positive effects on physiology, relieving or reversing some of the bad effects of the stress response. Humor and mirthful laughter increase natural killer cell activity and immunoglobulins, thus strengthening the neuroimmune system. Patients may differ with regard to the experiences and activities that elicit joy, humor and mirthful laughter. For example, some patients may enjoy telling jokes or reading comic books. Others might gain greater enjoyment from a comedy on screen. If a patient is to develop good humor skills, the capacity to experience periods of joy in the midst of adversity must be encouraged.

Positive respites provide opportunities for energy renewal, an essential ingredient in the stress recovery process. These respites are not intended to lead the patient into avoidance of reality. Rather, they are stress-reducing time-outs that provide the patient with a sense of release and renewal. There are several ways in which patients can seek these positive moments, such as spending time with a loved one or in a quiet location. The purpose of these respites is to recover and renew energy for constructively managing the inevitable and necessarily stressful dimensions of work and life.

Ten steps to staying healthy. Table 4.1 extends and elaborates these four basic skills into ten steps to staying healthy in times of high stress, trauma or tragedy. They are at the core of excellent self-care and good preventive stress management. The four basic skills and ten steps should serve as a firm foundation for building strength and managing vulnerability and risks.

Primary, secondary and tertiary prevention

The preventive management of stress is practiced at primary, secondary and tertiary levels. There is sometimes a tendency to focus on secondary prevention because it targets the individual's stress response. However, the preferred starting point is at a primary level. First, the stressors and trauma to which an individual is subjected should be examined. Next, or perhaps simultaneously, secondary prevention should be targeted. At this stage, consideration should be given to how the individual responds to the stressors. In theory, tertiary prevention should be a last resort. However, it is clearly an essential first course of action for those with obvious signs of strain, in whom some form of treatment or intervention will be necessary. In such cases, when the symptoms and signs of strain have been treated, a prevention plan, including primary and secondary prevention, should be developed.

A recognized set of primary, secondary and tertiary prevention methods have been researched extensively (Table 4.2). The physician can provide patients with behavioral guidelines for specific methods (see Chapters 5 and 6) and suggest appropriate books and resources,

TABLE 4.1

Ten steps to staying healthy in times of high stress

1. Remember to drink plenty of water and eat regular and healthy meals

2. Keep some physical activity in your routine

3. If the high-stress situation results from a tragedy, pace your exposure to media accounts or conversations about it. Plan how much time you need to watch, listen or read about the tragedy before taking a break

4. Breathe – deep breathing and relaxation practice are valuable ways to inoculate yourself against strain, especially during high-stress periods

5. If loss or tragedy causes the high stress, expect to go through a grieving process. Feelings will likely include rage, deep sadness, fear for safety, maybe even 'survivor's guilt'. Know that this is a natural process

6. It's a good idea to write down your deepest thoughts and feelings about highly stressful and/or traumatic events. Doing this for as little as 15–20 minutes will allow your emotions to settle and will facilitate healing

7. Take extra care to drive defensively and become especially focused in the moment as you drive. If the high-stress situation is affecting your whole community, remember that stress or fear may distract other drivers too

8. If you have religious beliefs, pray for others who are in the high stress situation with you – for those whose lives have been turned upside-down, for those responding to the trauma, and for leaders who need to make wise decisions and take action. Pray also for your physical, emotional and spiritual health in difficult times

9. Maintain your regular routine and healthy activities. Go about your work and your life without getting stuck in a rut. Act in defiance of other people attempting to control your life, by continuing to truly live

10. Watch for ways in which your mind or body is showing the tension it is experiencing as a result of the high stress. If appropriate, do not hesitate to call for professional help and guidance from a licensed or accredited healthcare specialist

Acknowledgement: adapted from guidelines compiled by Wayne Martin, Licensed Clinical Social Worker (LCSW), for use in clinical practice with people under stress, especially those in high-stress situations

TABLE 4.2

Primary, secondary and tertiary prevention methods

Prevention method	Specific aim
Primary prevention	
Learned optimism	Alters the individual's way of thinking about adversity and stressful events or people
Time management	Improves planning and prioritizing of activities and eliminates unnecessary activities
Modifying type A behavior	Reduces the anger, hostility and intensity associated with this behavior
Establishment of supportive relationships	Enhances resources, knowledge and support to manage stressors, stressful events and adversity
Secondary prevention	
Physical fitness	Improves cardiovascular strength and function, and improves muscle strength and flexibility
Relaxation training	Lowers all indicators of the stress response and provides calming skills for stressful times
Diet	Improves overall physical health and lowers the risk of cardiovascular disease and cancer
Emotional outlets	Provides releases for emotional stress and tension
Tertiary prevention	
Traumatic stress debriefings	Releases the emotional stress and conflicts resulting from trauma
Professional help	Provides medical (e.g. cardiology, oncology, psychiatry) treatment, drug therapy and psychological counseling to heal those with specific distress and strain problems

such as those included in the key references sections of this and the following chapter. The patient must practice the skills or methods on a regular basis. A single skill is not sufficient; people need a set of prevention and coping skills for successful stress management. Evidence shows that individuals who develop and practice two or more preventive stress management skills are able to cope significantly better than individuals who only practice one. It is also possible that patients will tailor stress management skills to tackle their specific stressors and stress. By charting stressors, stress responses and symptoms with time, patients and caregivers can discover the relative effectiveness of different management methods employed (Figure 4.2). Patients are

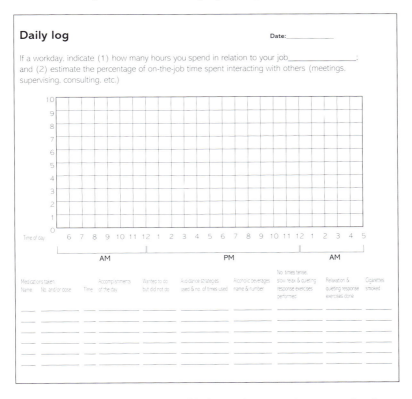

Figure 4.2 Completing a daily log will help a patient recognize stress-related symptoms and their associated behavior. As a result, strategies can be formulated for modifying behavior to manage stress better.

taught to recognize stress-related symptoms, such as anxiety, headache or muscular tension, and record their level of pain or discomfort, ranging from 1 (very low) to 10 (very high). The medical, psychological or behavioral responses of the patient will reflect the effectiveness of the management methods for that individual.

Key points – Preventive management of stress

- Stress is a chronic health risk that follows a natural history progressing from stressors, through the stress response, to frank strain.
- Natural strength or protective factors, as well as stress vulnerabilities and risk factors, vary from patient to patient.
- Basic skills for preventive stress management include diaphragmatic breathing, flexibility practices, humor and positive respites.
- Primary and secondary prevention skills help healthy patients enhance their stress coping capabilities.
- Tertiary prevention comprises treatment for patients in frank strain.

Key references

Eliot RS. *From Stress to Strength: How to Lighten your Load and Save your Life.* New York: Bantam Books, 1995.

Elkin AJ, Rosch PJ. Promoting mental health at the workplace: the prevention side of stress management. In: Scofield ME, ed. *Worksite Health Promotion.* Philadelphia: Hanley and Belfus, 1990:737–54. Also appears in *Occupational Medicine: State of the Art Reviews* 1990;5(4):739–54.

Rollins KL. *Wellness Center Workbook.* Fort Worth: Wellness Center, 1995.

Quick JC, Tetrick LE. *Handbook of Occupational Health Psychology.* Washington, DC: American Psychological Association, 2003.

5 Primary and secondary prevention methods

Primary and secondary prevention methods are long-term approaches to changing how an individual experiences, manages and responds to a wide range of stressors and trauma. These prevention methods require the patient to acquire some complex behavioral skills, which are not short-term solutions for acute stress-related problems. Primary and secondary prevention methods provide behavioral and psychological tools that enable individuals to develop self-reliance skills for the long-term, successful preventive management of stress. Some patients are likely to practice one or more of these primary and secondary skills already. The physician should consider prescribing one or two additional methods for the patient to develop. Suggesting more than two new prevention methods at any one time has been shown to significantly reduce successful integration of the practice into the patient's lifestyle.

Primary preventive management

Four methods for primary preventive stress management are:
- learned optimism
- time management and planning
- modifying type A behavior pattern
- building supportive social relationships.

These methods are complementary; each emphasizes a different aspect of the behavioral and psychological skills necessary for successful stress management. To achieve the greatest benefit, an individual should select and regularly practice one or two of the skills that are most appropriate for them.

Learned optimism. This psychological skill helps a person to modify their perceptions about events, primarily bad events and adversity, and to think positively instead. Individuals tend to develop either optimistic or pessimistic habits of thought with regard to life events. Optimistic thinkers focus on the benefits of good events and minimize the stressful aspects of bad events. These individuals view adversity as temporary, with limited bad effects, and something that is not their personal responsibility. In contrast, pessimistic habits of thought tend to magnify adversity and the stressful aspects of bad events, and minimize the benefits of good events. Pessimistic thinkers feel responsible for adversity and view it as more permanent and with wider-ranging consequences.

The aim of learned optimism is to change the way in which a person views life events, particularly adversity, and consequently to make bad events less stressful while increasing the experience of hope for the individual concerned. The patient should answer the questions in Table 5.1 and follow the suggestions for changing habits of thinking. More details for practice can be found in Seligman (1990).

The physician can prescribe diary writing for patients who may be pessimistic thinkers, as in Case report 2.1 (page 15). By recording thoughts and feelings at the end of each day for a minimum of 2 weeks and then reading through the diaries after a week's delay, a patient can see how pessimistic, or optimistic, their thinking may be. This initial knowledge is the important first step identified in Table 5.1. Pessimistic or negative thinking also manifests as worry, which is another form of dysfunctional beliefs and perceptions. Exercises, rules and prescriptions for patients who want to stop worrying can be found in the time-tested methods of Carnegie (1984/1944). His rules include: keep busy, don't sweat the small stuff, cooperate with the inevitable, and let the past die in peace.

Time management and planning are primary prevention skills that allow healthy achievement, while avoiding overload and a crisis management approach. Crisis managers create more stress both for themselves and for others around them. People who manage events in a broader context are macro time managers with skills to plan using a GP[3] approach (Goal setting, Prioritize, Plan, Praise; Table 5.2). Developed by Brooks and Mullins, this approach helps people set and prioritize goals, create and execute plans, and then feel good about achieving results. Personal goals are as important as professional goals. A further skill of good macro time managers is to recognize that goals

TABLE 5.1

Learning to think and behave optimistically

Identify your habits of thought

- When bad events happen and adversity strikes, do you think of it as permanent?
- Do you consider it to have bad effects on many parts of your life?

Identify the stressful effects of your thoughts

- Following bad events and adversity, do your bad feelings last a long time?
- Do you feel depressed and upset for a long time?

Choose the best way to change your habits of thought

- Two ways to develop more optimistic habits of thought are:
  - dispute pessimistic thoughts about adversity with evidence and alternatives
  - distract yourself from bad events by thinking about good events

Develop positive energy in new directions

- Focus your thoughts and energy on the good and positive events in your life
- Think about ways to expand and extend these good events

and priorities change with time, and that a failure to be flexible will lead to strain rather than to the healthy channeling of stress-induced energy. Perhaps the biggest benefit of setting goals and priorities is avoidance of chronic overload. Everyone experiences overloading at times, but chronic overload is a significant source of stress and therefore needs to be avoided.

Modifying type A behavior pattern. Type A behavior pattern is a socially and self-induced form of habitual behavior that induces stress. It is an individual difference that negatively influences the stress process. The key characteristics of this behavior pattern are:

- competitiveness
- a sense of urgency

47

TABLE 5.2

The GP³ approach to macro time management

Goal setting

- Set challenging, specific and measurable goals
- Let your natural desire shape your goals

Prioritize

- Some goals are more important than others
- Make the most important goals your top priority

Plan to achieve your goals

- Identify activities necessary to achieve your goals
- Schedule these activities with realistic deadlines
- Ask for help or delegate to others when appropriate

Praise yourself

- Talk and think positively
- Congratulate yourself as progress is achieved

- a quest for numbers, or quantities, of anything (e.g. money)
- a sense of insecurity
- aggression and hostility.

Individuals who do not exhibit these behaviors are considered to have type B personalities. To modify type A behavior, individuals need to learn new behaviors that will enable them to develop more self-control and be less hot-headed (Table 5.3). Controlling anger and hostility is a key skill for individuals who exhibit type A behavior. To help them achieve this, people with a tendency towards type A behavior should be encouraged to spend time with type B people, who can help them slow down and take stock of situations before reacting.

Building supportive social relationships. The absence of positive, supportive social relationships is a major health risk factor. Such relationships provide individuals with a range of resources, such as information, feedback and emotional caring, that have an important

TABLE 5.3

Modifying type A behavior

Ask 'Why am I in a hurry?'

- There are times when being in a hurry is warranted
- When it is not, slow down and take your time

Cool your anger

- Before you explode in a fit of temper, take a step back and a deep breath

Participate in non-competitive activities

- Both competitive and non-competitive activities are of value

role in the preventive management of stress. Individuals have varying needs for diversity and depth of social relationships. Major life changes may leave individuals with gaps in their social support systems. It is important to determine whether advice, feedback and emotional caring are available to individuals within their support system (Figure 5.1).

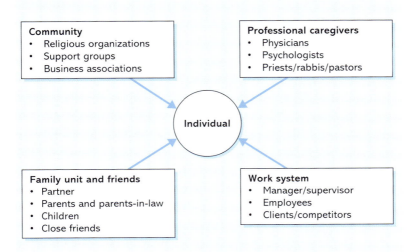

Figure 5.1 Secure, supportive relationships help people manage stressors and buffer them from strain.

TABLE 5.4

Guidelines for maintaining supportive social relationships

- Be honest and considerate in your communication
- Be prepared to apologize when appropriate
- Appreciate what you receive from the relationship
- Give willingly
- Listen fully to the other's ideas, thoughts and feelings
- When in conflict, affirm the person, if not the person's ideas or beliefs

Self-reliant people exhibit reciprocity, forming and maintaining supportive relationships with a number of other people, although it is likely that they will give more to some relationships and receive more from others. Following a set of guidelines can help individuals build and maintain positive, supportive relationships (Table 5.4).

Secondary preventive management

Four methods for secondary preventive stress management are:
- physical fitness
- relaxation training
- diet
- emotional outlets.

These methods provide behavioral and psychological supplements to the skills described for primary prevention of stress. Secondary prevention methods alter an individual's response to the everyday stressors of life. Maximum benefits are most likely to be achieved with long-term, regular practice of these skills.

Physical fitness involves two major systems of the body – the cardiovascular and musculoskeletal systems (Figure 5.2). Aerobic exercise, such as jogging, brisk walking, cycling or rowing, is a common way to achieve cardiovascular conditioning. Individuals will benefit from such activities if they achieve increased heart, respiration and metabolic rates for at least 20–30 minutes, three times a week (Table 5.5).

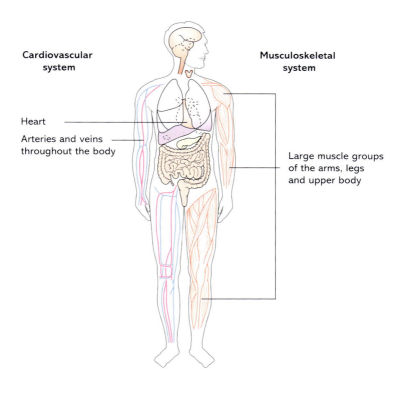

Cardiovascular system

Musculoskeletal system

Heart

Arteries and veins throughout the body

Large muscle groups of the arms, legs and upper body

Figure 5.2 The cardiovascular and musculoskeletal systems are the primary targets of physical fitness activities.

TABLE 5.5

The benefits of cardiovascular conditioning

- Resting heart rates are lowered by up to 23%
- Each heart beat has an increased blood volume
- Resting levels of catecholamines are lowered
- Action between the sympathetic and parasympathetic nervous systems is improved
- Recovery times following stressful events or activities are quicker

Case report 5.1

Dr J, aged 50 years, was chairman of a bank that was caught in a banking industry crisis. This bank ultimately failed. During the 24-month failure process, Dr J experienced mild stress-related symptoms, including periodic insomnia, and was diagnosed with mild anemia following the period of crisis. The patient's history revealed many protection factors and few vulnerability factors. A highly successful competitive swimmer, Dr J had a regular exercise regimen of swimming and running, which he maintained throughout the crisis. He had a happy, secure marriage and home life. He prayed regularly and had a strong management team. The two stress coping strategies he added during the crisis were diary writing and meeting with a small support group of entrepreneurs and corporate executives. The diary writing was an emotional outlet and enabled him to capture information that he later used to write a best-selling book. The support group of peers was able to offer Dr J emotional, psychological and material support, along with feedback and encouragement. In the group, he was able to overcome any social isolation from the loneliness of command and to express himself candidly and personally. This group added to an already strong set of supportive social relationships.

Muscle flexibility and weight training improve both the cardiovascular and musculoskeletal systems. These activities counter the bracing element (i.e. muscle tension and contraction) of the stress response. Muscle flexibility is achieved through rhythmic routines such as dance and stretching. Strength training may be key to managing specific stressors successfully. Strengthening exercises may be of particular benefit to elderly individuals to help them maintain muscle capacity and tone.

Relaxation training. The natural counterbalance to the stress response is the relaxation response (Figure 5.3). However, some people need to be taught how to elicit this. Relaxation training is the best way to

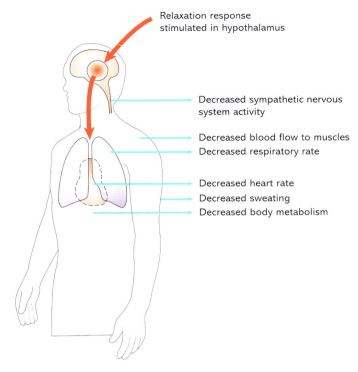

Relaxation response
stimulated in hypothalamus

Decreased sympathetic nervous
system activity

Decreased blood flow to muscles
Decreased respiratory rate

Decreased heart rate
Decreased sweating
Decreased body metabolism

Figure 5.3 Physiological changes associated with the relaxation response.

relearn relaxation, and includes a range of psychological and muscular relaxation methods designed to reverse the arousal effects of the stress response. Quick et al. (1997) describe several alternative relaxation practices. One simple procedure for relaxation can be practiced once or twice a day for 10–20 minutes (Table 5.6). Other methods for learning and practicing relaxation include peaceful prayer, meditation, progressive muscle relaxation and biofeedback. However, if these techniques are practiced too often or for too long in a single session, they may result in undesirable side effects, such as lethargy.

Diet contributes to a person's overall health and good dietary practices reduce vulnerability to strain. Diet plays an indirect role in stress; for example, high sugar levels can stimulate the stress response, while

TABLE 5.6

Guidelines for relaxation training

- Choose a peaceful place where you will not be disturbed
- Sit quietly in a comfortable position
- Close your eyes
- Relax your muscles
- Breathe slowly and naturally
- If appropriate, it may help to repeat silently to yourself a word from your spiritual tradition
- Be passive; let thoughts come and go without holding them
- Continue this process for up to 20 minutes; do not set an alarm
- When ready, open your eyes and become alert again

high cholesterol has an adverse effect on blood chemistry. A daily stress prevention diet would consist of 20% or less fat, 65–70% carbohydrate, 10–15% protein and 5 mg of cholesterol. Caffeine is also a stimulant for the stress response. People consuming more than 600 mg per day (about five or six cups of regular coffee) are at risk of becoming addicted; less than 300 mg per day is the recommended caffeine intake for adults. Doctors should recommend people eat balanced meals of grain (40%), vegetables (25%), legumes (20%), fruit (10%) and animal products (5%) at each sitting.

Emotional outlets. The release of stress-induced energy can be healthy. Some environments and relationships pose social barriers to emotional expression, so discretion and good judgment should be used when selecting appropriate situations for such expression. There are three particularly valuable emotional outlets:

- writing – personal diaries, which offer privacy, and letters, which should be used with discretion, are common forms of emotional expression
- talking – emotional expression in secure, supportive relationships is possibly one of the most cathartic and constructive means of addressing specific stressful events

- acting – by crying, laughing and shouting in appropriate settings, emotions can be legitimately expressed.

Expressive writing in private diaries is one of the most powerful and therapeutic forms of emotional expression for the preventive management of stress. Captain P (Case report 3.1, page 30) made effective use of expressive writing to reduce the generalized anxiety associated with the stress of major new job responsibilities. Dr J (Case report 5.1, page 52) similarly made effective use of expressive writing, in his case to manage the stress of a banking crisis. Such writing is a form of confession, and similar positive benefits can be gained from emotional expression to people with whom the patient has intimate, confidential relationships, such as a minister, psychologist, priest or close friend. It is the uninhibited expression of feeling and emotion that is important for healthy stress management.

If patients are to benefit from the emotional outlet of expressive writing, they should follow these specific steps.

1. Find a quiet, private place in which to write.
2. Use a notebook or computer which can be secured, so that it is not available to others.
3. Select a stressful experience or event from the present or past.
4. Write about this experience for 15–20 minutes.

Key points – Primary and secondary prevention methods

- Primary and secondary prevention skills extend, enhance and supplement the basic skills described in Chapter 4.
- Primary and secondary prevention skills aim to modify the causes of stress and enhance positive responses to inevitable stress.
- Primary prevention skills include learned optimism, time management and planning, modifying type A behavior and enhancing social supports.
- Secondary prevention skills include physical exercise, relaxation, prayer, diet and emotional outlets.

5. Freely express all of the feelings and emotions that surround this event.

At the end of the writing period, the patient should secure the notebook or computer, or destroy what has been written so that it is not available to anyone else, unless they choose to reveal what they have written.

Key references

Benson H, Stark M. *Timeless Healing: The Power and Biology of Belief*. New York: Scribner, 1996.

Brooks WT, Mullins TW. *High Impact Time Management*. Englewood Cliffs: Prentice-Hall, 1989.

Carnegie D. *How to Stop Worrying and Start Living*. New York: Pocket Books, 1984 [original work, 1944].

Cooper K. *The New Aerobics*. New York: Bantam Books, 1970.

Jacobson EJ. *Progressive Relaxation*. Chicago: University of Chicago, 1929.

Murphy LR. Stress management in work settings: a critical review of the research literature. *Am J Health Promot* 1996;11:112–35.

Ornish D. *Dr Dean Ornish's Program for Reversing Heart Disease*. New York: Ivy Books, 1990.

Pennebaker JW, Colder M, Sharp LK. Accelerating the coping process. *J Pers Soc Psychol* 1990;58:528–37.

Quick JD, Nelson DL, Matuszek PAC et al. Social support, secure attachments, and health. In: Cooper CL, ed. *Handbook of Stress, Medicine, and Health*. Boca Raton: CRC Press, 1996:269–87.

Roskies E. *Stress Management for the Healthy Type A: Theory and Practice*. New York: Guilford Press, 1987.

Seligman MEP. *Learned Optimism*. New York: Knopf, 1990.

Sutherland V, Cooper C. *Strategic Stress Management*. London: Macmillan Books, 2001.

Preventive stress management includes medical and psychological treatment by trained professionals, and self-care therapy. For patients who are stressed and/or strained, a balance of professional and self-help is likely to be the best approach. While healing is a natural process, there is significant benefit to be derived from help given by trained health professionals. The stigma still associated with stress-related disorders, such as anxiety, panic attacks and depression, may lead patients to resist seeking professional help. The role of the family physician is to provide short-term relief, serve as an educated resource and act as a valuable triage agent in partnership with mental health professionals to ensure that patients receive the necessary treatment. There is a range of interventions available for the most common forms of strain (Table 6.1).

Although a wide range of health professionals consider themselves to be stress experts, there is no single medical or psychological specialty with particular expertise in stress. For this reason, professional partnerships often provide the most effective approach to treating stress-related disorders.

Pharmacological intervention is most appropriate in the management of chronic, life-threatening stress-related problems, such as hypertension,

TABLE 6.1

Medical and psychological interventions for the preventive management of strain

Medical
- Pharmacotherapy
    - anxiolytics
    - antidepressants
- Physiotherapy
- Surgery

Psychological
- Psychotherapy
    - individual
    - group
- Behavior therapy
- Traumatic event debriefing

diabetes and cancer. Pharmacotherapy is also highly appropriate as adjunctive treatment for the most common stress-related anxiety and depressive problems. Osteopathic medicine can be used as a preventive measure to address some of the musculoskeletal correlates of these problems. Traditional Chinese medicine and Ayurveda, a traditional Hindu system of medicine based on balancing bodily systems, can be effective for a variety of musculoskeletal problems, digestive disorders and other self-limited conditions. Such approaches work together with the natural healing process. By understanding what can be achieved by appropriate treatment, individuals begin to accept responsibility for their own health, and that responsibility is an underlying principle of the most effective preventive management of stress.

Medical management

Pharmacotherapy is an important element of the medical management of strain (Table 6.2). Anxiety, nervousness, panic attacks and depression are among the most common symptoms of strain treated by primary care physicians in the USA, UK and many westernized countries.

Anxiolytics, such as diazepam, prescribed on a short-term basis, are most likely to benefit individuals experiencing periods of acute crisis, unusually severe stress or insomnia. Short term is usually taken to be a period of approximately 3 months. There are at least three difficulties associated with the long-term use of anxiolytics:

- such therapy can be addictive with complex withdrawal patterns
- the drugs may take the edge off a person's mental acuity and physical dexterity, making it hazardous for them to perform certain tasks
- patients may feel better in the short term, but the treatment may dampen an individual's motivation to find effective, permanent solutions.

Antidepressants, such as fluoxetine, can effectively alleviate depressive symptoms, particularly if used in combination with psychotherapy to address the psychological issues of the depression (Tables 6.3 and 6.4). As treatment for a major depression, antidepressants can provide highly effective short-term (3 months) therapy. They may also be required for long-term treatment. Patients

TABLE 6.2

Benzodiazepines commonly prescribed for anxiety

Drug	Daily dose (mg)	Rate of onset	Half-life (hours)
Alprazolam	0.75–4	Intermediate	6.3–26.9
Chlordiazepoxide	15–100	Intermediate	5–30
Clorazepate	15–60	Fast	40–50
Diazepam	4–40	Very fast	20–80
Lorazepam	2–4	Intermediate	10–20
Oxazepam	30–120	Slow	5–20

Source: *Drug Facts and Comparisons.* St Louis, MI: Facts and Comparisons, 2001.

should therefore be encouraged to consider antidepressant therapy as an adjunct to other medical and psychological interventions for the treatment of depression.

Physical therapy and physiotherapy have a role in the management of stress-related illnesses and injuries, which is often understated. Primarily, physiotherapy is appropriate for the management of muscle tension in the back, shoulders, neck and even legs. In the form of massage, physiotherapy helps to reduce the muscle tension and related pain associated with stress. Physiotherapy may be combined with muscle relaxants designed to reduce muscle contractions.

Surgical treatment for major manifestations of strain, such as cardiovascular disease and cancer, is only an option for serious and advanced disease stages. This approach is best used in combination with other medical and psychological assessments. The aim of these assessments is to determine whether more basic lifestyle, nutritional or behavioral changes could prevent the disease process from advancing.

Psychological management

As stress is a psychophysiological experience, the psychological management of stress and strain may complement other treatments or be the primary mode of treatment. Psychological management is of

Case report 6.1

Mr C, aged 40 years, was under the care of a cardiologist following two myocardial infarctions. He continued to complain of chest pains, for which the cardiologist could not find an organic or physiological basis, as well as other more generalized anxieties and discomforts. A stress diagnostic profile was developed by asking questions about his work activities and his home environment, and having Mr C complete stress diagnostic survey questionnaires. The profile provided no evidence of even moderate, let alone high, levels of stressors or pressure within the work or the home environment, with the minor exception of mild complaints about incoming phone calls at the office.

Mr C was thus reporting very low levels of stress at work and at home, and was under a standard regimen of care for his cardiovascular problems, which appeared to be going well. Nevertheless, he was reporting symptoms with no apparent physiological or environmental basis. This type of stressor–strain discrepancy suggests clinical psychological problems involving pathological dysfunctional beliefs and/or perceptions. Therefore, Mr C's case was referred to a clinical psychologist for in-depth psychological diagnosis, testing and treatment.

particular importance when the reported experience or evidence of stress and strain appears to be out of balance with the stressors confronting the individual. For patients whose chronic symptoms cannot be accounted for by external events, circumstances or life changes, psychological investigation is of the utmost importance. In this context, a psychological evaluation can distinguish between a normal range of responsiveness to stressors and trauma, and a wide range of psychological adjustment disorders.

Depending on the diagnosis, different psychological interventions are available and appropriate for psychological and/or medical strain.

TABLE 6.3

Antidepressant medications: starting and maximum daily doses

Medication (brand name®*)	Starting dose**	Maximum daily dose[†]
Tricyclic antidepressants		
Amitriptyline (*Elavil, Lentizol*)	50–100 mg h.s.	300 mg[‡]
Amoxapine (*Asendin*)	100–150 mg daily	600 mg
Clomipramine (*Anafranil*)	25 mg h.s.	250 mg
Desipramine (*Norpramin*)	25–100 mg h.s.	300 mg
Doxepin (*Sinequan*)	75 mg h.s.	300 mg
Imipramine (*Tofranil*)	75 mg h.s.	300 mg[§]
Nortriptyline (*Pamelor, Allegron*)	25 mg t.i.d.	150 mg
Protriptyline (*Vivactil*)	5 mg t.i.d.	60 mg
Trimipramine (*Surmontil*)	50–75 mg daily	300 mg[§]
Atypical antidepressants		
Bupropion (*Wellbutrin, Zyban*)	100 mg b.i.d.	450 mg
Maprotiline (*Ludiomil*)	25–75 mg daily	225 mg
Mirtazapine (*Remeron, Zispin*)	15 mg h.s.	45 mg
Nefazodone (*Serzone, Dutonin*)	100 mg b.i.d.	600 mg
Trazodone (*Desyrel, Molipaxin*)	150 mg daily	400 mg[¶]
Venlafaxine (*Effexor, Efexor*)	37.5 mg b.i.d.	375 mg
Selective serotonin reuptake inhibitors		
Citalopram (*Celexa, Cipramil*)	20 mg daily	60 mg
Fluoxetine[#] (*Prozac*)	20 mg daily	80 mg
Fluvoxamine (*Faverin*)	50 mg h.s.	300 mg
Paroxetine (*Paxil, Seroxat*)	20 mg daily	60 mg
Sertraline (*Zoloft, Lustral*)	50 mg daily	200 mg

b.i.d., twice daily; h.s., at bedtime; t.i.d., three times daily.
*Brand names may vary by country; common brand names in USA and UK are listed.
**Doses may vary from patient to patient depending on age, gender, severity of condition and other factors. Doses should be adjusted appropriately.
[†]Reduce dose in the elderly.
[‡]In hospital patients only, otherwise 150 mg.
[§]In hospital patients only, otherwise 200 mg.
[¶]600 mg daily can be given to inpatients in divided doses.
[#]Also available in a weekly dose of 90 mg.
Data on doses from http://ePocrates.com; accessed November 2002.

TABLE 6.4

Common side effects of antidepressant medications

Medication	Agitation	Sedation	Hypotension	Anticholinergic effects
Tricyclic antidepressants*				
Amitriptyline	0	3+	3+	3+
Amoxapine	0	+	2+	+
Clomipramine	0	2+	2+	3+
Desipramine	+	0/+	+	+
Doxepin	0	3+	2+	2+
Imipramine	0/+	2+	2+	2+
Nortriptyline	0	+	+	+
Protriptyline	2+	0/+	+	2+
Atypical antidepressants				
Bupropion	3+	0	0	0
Maprotiline	0/+	2+	2+	2+
Mirtazapine	0	4+	0/+	0
Nefazodone	0	3+	0	0
Trazodone	0	3+	0	0
Venlafaxine	0/+	0	0	0
Selective serotonin reuptake inhibitors				
Citalopram	0/+	0/+	0	0
Fluoxetine	+	0/+	0	0
Fluvoxamine	0	0/+	0	0
Paroxetine	+	0/+	0	0/+
Sertraline	+	0/+	0	0

0, negligible; 0/+, minimal; +, mild; 2+, moderate; 3+, moderately severe; 4+, severe
*Side effects of trimipramine are generally similar to those for amitriptyline; please consult prescribing information
From: Miller KE, Zylestra RG, Standridge JB. *Depression. Monograph 284. AAFP Home Study.* Leawood, Kansas: American Academy of Family Physicians, 2003:32. Adapted by AAFP authors from Baldessarini RJ. Drugs and the treatment of psychiatric disorders: depression and anxiety disorders. In: Hardman JG, Limbird LE, Gilman AG, eds. *Goodman & Gilman's: The Pharmacological Basis of Therapeutics.* 10th ed. New York, NY: McGraw-Hill; 2001:447–483. Reproduced with permission of The McGraw-Hill Companies.

Gastrointestinal effects	Weight gain	Sexual effects	Cardiac effects
0/+	2+	2+	3+
0/+	+	2+	2+
+	2+	3+	3+
0/+	+	2+	2+
0/+	2+	2+	3+
0/+	2+	2+	3+
0/+	+	2+	2+
0/+	+	2+	3+
2+	0	0	0
0/+	+	2+	2+
0/+	0/+	0	0
2+	0/+	0/+	0/+
2+	+	+	0/+
3+	0	3+	0/+
3+	0	3+	0
3+	0/−	3+	0/+
3+	0	3+	0
3+	0/+	3+	0
3+	0	3+	0

Psychotherapy. Most forms of psychotherapy are based on a psychodynamic model of people, which relies on insight, psychological understanding and the individual's own responsibility for managing stress and making life changes. Brief psychotherapy may be used in combination with medical or surgical treatment to enhance the healing process in those who experience violent trauma. Research suggests that psychologists, psychiatrists and social workers are equally effective in providing psychotherapy services, and that all three are more effective for this type of psychological management than marriage counselors and family physicians. The physician has the important role of referring patients, as appropriate, for psychological diagnosis and management or for psychotherapy.

Behavior therapy places greater emphasis on achieving demonstrable changes in behavior and less emphasis on the psychological understanding of the individual and the events in their life. Behavior therapy relies on the important principle of counter-conditioning, the process of unlearning old reaction patterns by practicing more desirable ones. There are two common types of behavior therapy:
- systematic desensitization, which generalizes the relaxation response to situations an individual finds to be stressful
- self-reinforcement, which positively reinforces desirable behaviors and behavior change through the use of rewards.

Controlled research has shown significant positive results for the use of systematic desensitization. Although useful for changing specific behaviors, behavior therapy is less appropriate for general anxiety, adjustment or adaptation problems, or for individuals with personality disorders.

Traumatic event debriefing is highly appropriate in cases of violent events, physical aggression and harassment, unexpected loss of a loved one or job, and other trauma. Traumatic event debriefing is useful as a treatment intervention to prevent PTSD, combat stress reactions (CSR) and heart-of-darkness syndrome. Heart-of-darkness syndrome is characterized by feelings of vulnerability, lack of empathy for the enemy and a positive attitude toward killing. Traumatic event debriefing is also appropriate for professionals and caregivers managing traumatic events, such as bombings and natural disasters. In such situations, professional caregivers are subject to secondary traumatic stress. This psychological management is a form of confessional that can aid the healing process if used alongside other emotional outlets.

Key points – Medical and psychological treatment

- Tertiary prevention includes medical and psychological treatment for those with frank strain.
- Treatment should aim to reduce symptoms and then to focus on the development of basic and supplementary preventive skills.
- Medical treatment includes pharmacotherapy, physical therapy or physiotherapy and, in the extreme, surgery.
- Psychological treatment includes psychotherapy, behavioral therapy and traumatic event debriefing. The objective of treatment is self-regulation and self-control during stressful times.

Key references

Busuttil A, Busuttil W. Psychological debriefing. *Br J Psychiatry* 1995;166: 676–7.

Katerndahl DA. Anxiety disorders. In: Taylor RB et al., eds. *Family Medicine: Principles and Practice.* 4th edn. New York: Springer-Verlag, 1994:224–33.

Kiecolt-Glaser JK, Glaser R. Psychoneuroimmunology and health consequences: data and shared mechanisms. *Psychosomatic Med* 1995;57:269–74.

Miller JA. Traumatic event debriefing: Comment. *Social Work* 1995;40:576.

Ravindran AV, Griffiths J, Waddell C et al. Stressful life events and coping styles in relation to dysthymia and major depressive disorder: Variations associated with alleviation of symptoms following pharmacotherapy. *Progress Neuropsychopharmacol Biol Psychiatry* 1995;19:637–53.

Rosenbaum JF. The drug treatment of anxiety. *N Engl J Med* 1982;306: 401–4.

Seligman MEP. The effectiveness of psychotherapy: The Consumer Reports Study. *Am Psychol* 1995; 50:965–74.

Van Os J, Fahy TA, Bebbington PE et al. The influence of life events on the subsequent course of psychotic illness: A prospective follow-up of the Camberwell Collaborative Psychosis Study. *Psychol Med* 1994;24;503–13.

Williams GO. Management of depression in the elderly. *Primary Care* 1989;16:451–74.

Stress is a valuable source of energy to manage legitimate emergencies and achieve peak performance, particularly in physical tasks and athletic events. However, chronic or frequent intense experiences of stress pose a risk of a wide range of medical, psychological and behavioral health disorders. Stress plays a direct or contributing role in seven of the ten leading causes of death in developed nations. It plays an integral role in most chronic diseases and disorders. Most chronic health disorders require a more holistic approach to management, and physician–patient partnerships for self-care and treatment. Improved self-care through the preventive management of stress provides a window of opportunity for the future. Current stress research in Western countries focuses on the role of environmental characteristics and individual differences in stress-related disorders; future research should focus on holistic approaches to stress-related chronic disorders, and on treatment and intervention earlier in life.

Environmental characteristics and stress

Much stress research in developed nations focuses on the characteristics of work and home environments that cause stress-related disorders and disabilities. In some developed nations, over 10% of the labor force is on extended or permanent stress leave. The key elements of a person's overall environment are:
- their family unit
- the work system
- the community.

The latest research identifies three work system characteristics as the major stress risk factors for individuals: lack of control, uncertainty and conflict. The work system is a major source of stress for employed people, and also for their families, because of the effects of work stress being brought into the home environment. Companies have become increasingly aware of the importance of stress as a legitimate concern for managers and employees, even addressing the potential stress and conflict associated with the work–home interface. Senior executives acknowledge stress in the workplace, and many companies now employ counselors to advise employees.

Individual differences in stress

A second major area of stress research focuses on individual differences in stress response and vulnerability. In Chapter 2, four individual differences were discussed that either create vulnerability for or protection against stress-related disorders: gender, type A behavior pattern (stress propensity), family history and emotional intelligence. Research has also shown that two personality variables, personality hardiness and self-reliance, can moderate the stress process.

Two promising areas of research into individual differences concern gender and emotional intelligence. Recent work identifying the tend-and-befriend response in women under stress also has important implications for men's positive coping responses when stressed. The tend-and-befriend response is the instinct to form secure, positive attachments during stressful times or events. If men learn how to shift gears from fight-or-flight to tend-and-befriend, they too can benefit from secure, positive attachments.

Research into the role of emotional intelligence in the stress process is still in its infancy. While Cannon identified rage as one of the key emotions to ignite the stress response, more recent investigators have shown the constructive value of well-managed anger. This positive use of anger comes through emotional intelligence and self-regulation, both of which we need to learn more about in further stress research.

Holistic approaches to stress-related chronic disorders

While the importance of stress in chronic diseases and disorders is well understood, the specific contribution of stress in each of these problems is not well defined. Future research might apportion the contribution of causal and contributing factors to each of the major stress-related disorders. In addition, research into more holistic and alternative approaches to the preventive management of stress and strain is needed.

Future research should also focus on the effectiveness of partnering arrangements among professionals in the treatment of stress-related problems. Since chronic disorders have to be lived with for extended periods, there is a real opportunity for long-term treatment research evaluations.

Early age treatment and intervention

Many stress-related disorders, such as anxiety and depression, have roots in the individual's early life. Future research should focus on the effect of developing stress hardiness and self-reliance skills at a younger age as a defense against stress-related disorders in later life. Because many preventive management skills are life-long disciplines or habits, the cost-effectiveness of learning these skills early should be established. This line of research will help to identify the appropriate age at which various stress management skills would best be taught, and the most effective methods for preventive stress management.

TABLE 7.1

A simple set of guidelines remind the professional caregiver to practice preventive stress management

- Live with purpose and mission

- Keep your priorities clear and limited

- Focus on the good things in life, without ignoring the bad

- When angry, ask yourself – is it really justified?

- Take regular physical exercise

- Relax once or twice a day

- Express your positive emotions daily, but pause before verbally expressing the emotions that trouble you most, expressing them only in a spirit of kindness and forgiveness

- Ask for help, advice and counseling freely. You are not the center of the universe

Professional caregivers: leading the way

Professional caregivers are at risk of stress and burnout if they neglect
their own needs. By adhering to good preventive stress management
techniques, professional caregivers can be role models for their patients.
A simple set of guidelines is all that these health professionals may need
(Table 7.1). 'Doctor, heal thyself! ... and manage thy own stress' may
not be a panacea, but it is a positive first step.

Useful addresses

UK

British Association for
Counselling and Psychotherapy
BACP House
35–37 Albert Street
Rugby
Warwickshire
CV21 2SG
Tel: + 44 (0)870 443 5252
e-mail: bacp@bacp.co.uk
http://www.bacp.co.uk

**International Stress Management
Association**
Gordon House
83–85 Gordon Avenue
Stanmore, Middlesex
HA7 3QR
e-mail: info@csa-stress.co.uk

The Samaritans
Kingston Road
Ewell
Surrey
KT17 2AF
+ 44 (0)20 8394 8300 (admin)
e-mail: admin@samaritans.org
+44 (0) 8457 909090 (helpline)
e-mail: jo@samaritans.org
http://www.samaritans.org

International

International Society for the
Investigation of Stress
Professor G Burrows, Department
of Psychiatry
Melbourne University, Australia
e-mail: gdb@unimelb.edu.au

USA

American Institute of Stress
124 Parks Avenue
Yonkers
NY 10703
Tel: +1 914 963 1200
http://www.stress.org/
e-mail: stress124@earthlink.net

**Department of Health Education
and Welfare**
Office of Health Information and
Promotion
721B Hubert Humphrey Building
200 Independence Avenue SW
Washington, DC 20201
Tel: +1 202 205 8611
http://odphp.osophs.dhhs.gov

**National Mental Health
Association**
2001 N Beauregard Street
12th Floor
Alexandria, VA 22311
Tel: +1 703 684 7722
http://www.nmha.org/

**Employee Assistance Professionals
Association**
2101 Wilson Boulevard
Suite 500, Arlington
VA 22201
Tel: +1 703 387 1000
http://www.eap-association.org

**National Council on Alcoholism
and Drug Dependence**
20 Exchange Place, Suite 2902
New York, NY 10005-3201
Tel: +1 212 269 7797
Fax: +1 212 269 7510
e-mail:
communications@ncadd.org
http://www.ncadd.org

Index